57-6346

D1545932

THE GREEN WALL

Volume 53 of the
Yale Series of Younger Poets
Edited by W. H. Auden and
published on the
Mary Cady Tew
Memorial Fund

JAMES WRIGHT: THE

With a Foreword by W. H. AUDEN

GREEN WALL

New Haven: YALE UNIVERSITY PRESS, 1957

London: Oxford University Press

37665

Acknowledgments

For permission to reprint many of these poems, the author wishes to thank the editors of the following publications: *Harper's Bazaar, The University of Kansas City Review, The Sewanee Review, Assay, Audience, The Kenyon Review, Poetry: A Magazine of Verse, Hika, The Avon Book of Modern Writing No. 1, The Pacific Spectator, The Saturday Review, The Hudson Review, New World Writing No. 9, The Quarterly Review of Literature, The Western Review, The New Yorker, The Atlantic Monthly, Truth* (England), *The Paris Review* (France), and *Botteghe oscure* (Italy).

FOR TWO TEDS AND TWO JACKS

Foreword

Consciously or unconsciously, every poet draws a frontier between the poetical and the nonpoetical; certain objects, persons, events seem to him capable of embodiment in a poem, even if he has not yet discovered how, while there are others which it would never occur to him to consider himself, whatever other poets may have done with them. Further, among the various moods of feeling of which he is capable, he has preferences as a poet which may have little to do with his preferences as a man; a feeling which he enjoys may make little appeal to his imagination; a state of unpleasure may excite it.

Some of these distinctions are peculiar to himself, but most he shares with his contemporaries. From time to time a poet or a group of poets proclaim that the existing frontier is unjust and should be redrawn; when this happens, a new "period" of poetry begins.

One of the problems for a poet living in a culture with a well developed technology is that the history of technology is one of perpetual revolution, whereas genuine revolutions in the history of art (or society) are few and far between. He is tempted to imagine that, unless he produces something completely novel, he will be unoriginal. The reading public, too, may be similarly misled and attach undue importance to the individual differences between one poet and another, which, of course, exist and matter, ignoring that which is characteristic of them all, though this may really be of greater interest.

For example, Mr. Wright uses as an epigraph to this volume the well known medieval carol "Adam Lay Ibounden." It is as impossible to imagine a poet of the twentieth-century writing this as to imagine a fifteenth-century poet writing these lines by Mr. Wright:

> She was aware of scavengers in holes
> Of stone, she knew the loosened stones that fell
> Indifferently as pebbles plunging down a well
> And broke for the sake of nothing human souls.

A modern poet might perfectly well be a Catholic, believing in the Divine plan for human redemption of which the medieval carol sings, but his consciousness of historical earthly time is so different that he could never strike the same note of naïve joy in the present; should he attempt it, the note struck would almost certainly be false, expressing not Christian hope but a sort of Rotarian optimism.

A medieval poet, on the other hand, might have written an elegy on the death of a friend, though he would be more likely to choose a public figure, but it would never have occurred to him to celebrate the melancholia of the deceased; he would have described her beauty, her actions, he might even have portrayed her as a mourner, provided that the reason was some objective suffering, but a subjective illness like melancholia would have seemed to him unpoetic.

One way of perceiving the characteristics of an age is to raise certain fundamental questions which human beings have always asked and then see how the poets of that age answer them, such questions, for example as:

What is the essential difference between man and all the other creatures, animal, vegetable, and mineral?

What is the nature and human significance of time?

What qualities are proper to the hero or sacred person who can inspire poets to celebrate him and what is lacking in the churl or profane person whom poetry ignores?

A man in the Middle Ages would have said that the difference between man and other creatures is that only man has an immortal soul eternally related to God. He has, therefore, a goal, salvation or damnation, but this goal is not in time nor is reaching it a matter of time. A baby who has been baptized and an old man who repents after a lifetime of crime die and both are saved; their ages are irrelevant.

On the other hand, so far as his temporal existence, individual or social was concerned, like anyone who lives in a predominantly rural culture without machinery, he would be conscious of little difference between himself and other creatures, that is to say, he would be mainly aware of their common subjection to biological time, the endless cycle of birth, growth, and decay. Of man as creating irreversible historical time so that the next generation is never a repetition of the last, he would be scarcely, if at all, conscious. But to a modern man, whether or not he believes in an immortal soul, this is the great difference, that he and his society have a self-made history while the rest of nature does not. He is anxious by necessity because at every moment he has to choose to become himself. His typical feelings about nature, therefore are feelings of estrangement and nostalgia. In "A Fit against the Country" Mr. Wright sees nature as a temptation to try and escape human responsibility by imitating her ways, in "The Seasonless" he contrasts the rotation of the seasons with a human figure to whom no season can ever return, in "The Horse" and "On the Skeleton of a Hound" he contrasts the "poetical" animal and its unchanging identity with the "unpoetical" man who can never say who he is.

Poets have always reflected on the passage of time, comparing the present and the past, but before the modern period this usually meant expressing a sorrow because the present was less valuable than the past, what was once strong is now weak, what was beautiful has faded, and so forth, but past and present were felt to be equally real. But in Mr. Wright's poems, as in nearly all modern poetry, the present is not unhappy but unreal, and it is memories, pleasant or unpleasant, which are celebrated for their own sake as the real past. The present can only be celebrated, as in "A Girl in a Window" or "To a Hostess Saying Good Night," by showing it as pure chance; what makes the present moment poetical is an awareness that it is related to nothing so that nothing can come of it.

Two of Mr. Wright's poems, "The Assignation" and "My Grandmother's Ghost," are about the dead coming back to haunt the living.

In earlier times the motive for doing this would have been malignant and ghosts were regarded as evil. The good dead were thought to be much too happy in their present state to wish to return to their earthly life; in their thoughts about those on earth whom they had loved they looked not backward but forward to the future when their loved ones would join them. On earth past and present had seemed equally real; in eternity both seem equally unreal.

Given the circumstances of modern life, the feeling that only memories are real is to be expected. When a man usually lived in the house where his father and grandfather had lived before him, the past still existed in the present, not just as his memories but objectively about him. Today when men change not only their house but their part of the world every few years, their present circumstances become more and more impersonal, subjective memories more and more important.

Even more striking than its attitude toward nature and time is the kind of person whom modern poetry chooses to speak of. Aside from love poems and poems addressed to relatives, the persons who have stimulated Mr. Wright's imagination include a lunatic, a man who has failed to rescue a boy from drowning, a murderer, a lesbian, a prostitute, a police informer, and some children, one of them deaf. Common to them all is the characteristic of being social outsiders. They play no part in ruling the City nor is its history made by them, nor, even, are they romantic rebels against its injustices; either, like the children (and the ghosts), they are not citizens or they are the City's passive victims.

His one poem to a successful citizen is, significantly, to a singer, that is to say, to someone whose social function is concerned with the play of the City, not with its work.

Mr. Wright is not alone in his imaginative preferences.

It is difficult to find a modern poem, unless it be a satire, which celebrates a contemporary equivalent of Hector or Aeneas or King Arthur or the Renaissance Prince. To the poetic imagination of our time, it would seem that the authentically human, the truly strong, is someone who to the outward eye is weak or a failure, the only exception being the artist or the intellectual discoverer, the value of whose achievements is independent of his contemporary fame.

There are many reasons for this change, and everyone will be able to think of some for himself. One, obviously, is the impersonal character of modern public life which has become so complex that the personal contribution of any one individual is impossible to identify and even the greatest statesman seems more an official than a man. Another, I think, is the change effected by modern methods of publicity in the nature of fame. Formerly a man was famous *for* something, for this great deed or that which he had done; that is to say, the deed was the important thing and the name of the doer was, in a sense, an accident. Today a famous man is a man whose name is on everybody's lips. Their knowledge of what he has done may be very vague and its value, whether it was noble or shameful, matters very little. So long as he is in the news, he is a famous man; the moment he ceases to have news value, he becomes nobody.

We should not be surprised, then, if modern poets should be drawn to celebrate persons of whom nobody has heard or whom, at least, everybody has forgotten.

I have not said anything about the quality of Mr.

Wright's poems because assertions have no point without proofs, and the only proof in this case is reading. I will content myself with one or two quotations to illustrate his handling of imagery and rhythm and the variety of his concerns.

> Behind us, where we sit by trees,
> Blundering autos lurch and swerve
> On gravel, crawling on their knees
> Around the unfamiliar curve . . .

❧

> . . . The flop of wings, the jerk of the red comb
> Were a dumb agony,
> Stupid and meaningless. It was no joy
> To leave the body beaten underfoot;
> Life was a flick of corn, a steady roost.
> Chicken. The sound is plain.

❧

> And through the windows, washing hands,
> The patients have the mattress made,
> Their trousers felt for colored stones,
> The pleasures of the noon recalled:
>
> For some were caught and held for hours
> By spiders skating over a pond,
> Some parted veils of hollyhocks
> And looked for rabbit holes beyond.
>
> But now the trousers lie in rows,
> She sees the undressed shadows creep
> Through half-illuminated minds
> And chase the hare and flower to sleep.

But now I fumble at the single joy
Of dawn. On the pale ruffle of the lake
The ripples weave a color I can bear.
Under a hill I see the city sleep
And fade. The perfect pleasure of the eyes:
A tiny bird bathed in a bowl of air,
Carving a yellow ripple down the bines,
Posing no storm to blow my wings aside
As I drift upward dropping a white feather.

W. H. Auden

Contents

I. SCENES AND LAMENTS

A Fit against the Country   3
The Seasonless   5
The Horse   7
The Fishermen   9
A Girl in a Window   11
On the Skeleton of a Hound   12
Three Steps to the Graveyard   14
Father   16
Elegy in a Firelit Room   17
Arrangements with Earth for Three Dead Friends   19
Lament for My Brother on a Hayrake   21
She Hid in the Trees from the Nurses   22

II. TO TROUBLED FRIENDS

To a Defeated Saviour   27
To a Troubled Friend   29
Poem for Kathleen Ferrier   30
A Song for the Middle of the Night   32
A Presentation of Two Birds to My Son   34
To a Hostess Saying Good Night   36
A Poem about George Doty in the Death House   37
To a Fugitive   39

III. LOVES

Eleutheria   43
Autumnal   45
The Ungathered Apples   46
The Shadow and the Real   48
Witches Waken the Natural World in Spring   49
Morning Hymn to a Dark Girl   50
The Quail   52

IV. STORIES AND VOICES

Three Speeches in a Sick Room   57
Sappho   63
A Gesture by a Lady with an Assumed Name   67
Mutterings over the Crib of a Deaf Child   68
Crucifixion on Thursday   70
The Angel   72
The Assignation   75
Come Forth   79
Erinna to Sappho   81
The Three Husbands   83

V.

A Little Girl on Her Way to School   87
A Call from the Front Porch   89
My Grandmother's Ghost   91

Adam lay ibounden,
Bounden in a bond;
Four thousand winter
Thought he not too long.

And all was for an appil,
An appil that he tok,
As clerkes finden
Written in their book.

Ne had the appil take ben,
The appil take ben,
Ne hadde never our lady
A ben hevene quene.

Blessed be the time
That appil take was.
Therefore we moun singen
Deo gracias.

I SCENES AND LAMENTS

A Fit against the Country

The stone turns over slowly,
Under the side one sees
The pale flint covered wholly
With whorls and prints of leaf.
After the moss rubs off
It gleams beneath the trees,
Till all the birds lie down.
Hand, you have held that stone.

The sparrow's throat goes hollow,
When the tense air forebodes
Rain to the sagging willow
And leaves the pasture moist.
The slow, cracked song is lost
Far up and down wet roads,
Rain drowns the sparrow's tongue.
Ear, you have heard that song.

Suddenly on the eye
Feathers of morning fall,
Tanagers float away
To sort the blackberry theft.
Though sparrows alone are left
To sound the dawn, and call
Awake the heart's gray dolor,
Eye, you have seen bright color.

Odor of fallen apple
Met you across the air,
The yellow globe lay purple
With bruises underfoot;
And, ravished out of thought,
Both of you had your share,
Sharp nose and watered mouth,
Of the dark tang of earth.

Yet, body, hold your humor
Away from the tempting tree,
The grass, the luring summer
That summon the flesh to fall.
Be glad of the green wall
You climbed across one day,
When winter stung with ice
That vacant paradise.

The Seasonless

When snows begin to fill the park,
It is not hard to keep the eyes
Secure against the flickering dark,
Aware of summer ghosts that rise.
The blistered trellis seems to move
The memory toward root and rose,
The empty fountain fills the air
With spray that spangled women's hair;
And men who walk this park in love
May bide the time of falling snows.

The trees recall their greatness now;
They were not always vague and bowed
With loads that build the slender bough
Till branches bear a tasteless fruit.
A month ago they rose and bore
Fleshes of berry, leaf, and shade:
How painlessly a man recalls
The stain of green on crooked walls,
The summer never known before,
The garden heaped to bloom and fade.

Beyond the holly bush and path
The city lies to meet the night,
And also there the quiet earth
Relies upon the lost delight
To rise again and fill the dark
With waterfalls and swallows' sound.

Beyond the city's lazy fume,
The sea repeats the fall of spume,
And gulls remember cries they made
When lovers fed them off the ground.

But lonely underneath a heap
Of overcoat and crusted ice,
A man goes by, and looks for sleep,
The spring of everlastingness.
Nothing about his face revives
A longing to evade the cold.
The night returns to keep him old,
And why should he, the lost and lulled,
Pray for the night of vanished lives,
The day of girls blown green and gold?

The Horse

... the glory of his nostrils is terrible.
Job 39:20

He kicked the world, and lunging long ago
Rose dripping with the dew of lawns,
Where new wind tapped him to a frieze
Against a wall of rising autumn leaves.
Some young foolhardy dweller of the barrows,
To grip his knees around the flanks,
Leaped from a tree and shivered in the air.
Joy clawed inside the bones
And flesh of the rider at the reins
Flopping and bounding over the dark banks.

Joy and terror floated on either side
Of the rider rearing. The supreme speed
Jerked to a height so spaced and wide
He seemed among the areas of the dead.
The flesh was free, the sky was rockless, clear,
The road beneath the feet was pure, the soul
Spun naked to the air
And lanced against a solitary pole
Of cumulus, to curve and roll
With the heave that disdains
Death in the body, stupor in the brains.

Now we have coddled the gods away.
The cool earth, the soft earth, we say:
Cover our eyes with petals, let the sky

7

Drift on while we are watching water pass
Among the drowsing mass
Of red and yellow algae in green lanes.
Yet earth contains
The horse as a remembrancer of wild
Arenas we avoid.

One day a stallion whirled my riding wife,
Whose saddle rocked her as a cradled child,
Gentle to the swell of water; yet her life
Poised perilously as on a shattered skiff.
The fear she rode, reminded of the void
That flung the ancient rider to the cold,
Dropped her down. I tossed my reins,

I ran to her with breath to make her rise,
And brought her back. Across my arms
She fumbled for the sunlight with her eyes.
I knew that she would never rest again,
For the colts of the dusk rear back their hooves
And paw us down, the mares of the dawn stampede
Across the cobbled hills till the lights are dead.
Here it is not enough to pray that loves
Draw grass over our childhood's lake of slime.
Run to the rocks where horses cannot climb,
Stable the daemon back to the shaken earth,
Warm your hands at the comfortable fire,
Cough in a dish beside a wrinkled bed.

The Fishermen

We tossed our beer cans down among the rocks,
And walked away.
We turned along the beach to wonder
How many girls were out to swim and burn.
We found old men:

The driftwood faces
Sprawled in the air
And patterned hands half hidden in smoke like ferns;
The old men, fishing, letting the sea fall out,
Their twine gone slack.

You spoke of saurian beards
Grown into layers of lime,
Of beetles' shards and broad primeval moths
Lashing great ferns;
Of bent Cro-Magnon mothers beating
Their wheat to mash;
And salty stones
Stuck to the fin and scale
Of salmon skeleton,
And lonely fabulous whorls of wood
Drawn to the shore,
The carping nose, the claws, not to be known
From those dried fishermen:

Who watched the speedboat swaying in the scum
A mile offshore,
Or, nearer, leaping fish
Butting the baby ducks before their climb;
And last of all, before the eyes of age,
The calves of graceful women flashing fast
Into the fluffy towels and out of sight.

You pointed with a stick, and told me
How old men mourning the fall
Forget the splendid sea-top combed as clean as bone,
And the white sails.
You showed me how their faces withered
Even as we looked down
To find where they left off and sea began.

And though the sun swayed in the sea,
They were not moved:
Saurian faces still as layered lime,
The nostrils ferned in smoke behind their pipes,
The eyes resting in whorls like shells on driftwood,
The hands relaxing, letting out the ropes;
And they, whispering together,
The beaten age, the dead, the blood gone dumb.

A Girl in a Window

Now she will lean away to fold
The window blind and curtain back,
The yellow arms, the hips of gold,
The supple outline fading black,
Bosom availing nothing now,
And rounded shadow of long thighs.
How can she care for us, allow
The shade to blind imagined eyes?

Behind us, where we sit by trees,
Blundering autos lurch and swerve
On gravel, crawling on their knees
Around the unfamiliar curve;
Farther behind, a passing train
Ignores our lost identity;
So, reassured, we turn again
To see her vanish under sky.

Soon we must leave her scene to night,
To stars, or the indiscriminate
Pale accidents of lantern light,
A watchman walking by too late.
Let us return her now, my friends,
Her love, her body to the grave
Fancy of dreams where love depends.
She gave, and did not know she gave.

On the Skeleton of a Hound

Nightfall, that saw the morning-glories float
Tendril and string against the crumbling wall,
Nurses him now, his skeleton for grief,
His locks for comfort curled among the leaf.
Shuttles of moonlight weave his shadow tall,
Milkweed and dew flow upward to his throat.
Now catbird feathers plume the apple mound,
And starlings drowse to winter up the ground.
Thickened away from speech by fear, I move
Around the body. Over his forepaws, steep
Declivities darken down the moonlight now,
And the long throat that bayed a year ago
Declines from summer. Flies would love to leap
Between his eyes and hum away the space
Between the ears, the hollow where a hare
Could hide; another jealous dog would tumble
The bones apart, angry, the shining crumble
Of a great body gleaming in the air;
Quivering pigeons foul his broken face.
I can imagine men who search the earth
For handy resurrections, overturn
The body of a beetle in its grave;
Whispering men digging for gods might delve
A pocket for these bones, then slowly burn
Twigs in the leaves, pray for another birth.
But I will turn my face away from this
Ruin of summer, collapse of fur and bone.

For once a white hare huddled up the grass,
The sparrows flocked away to see the race.
I stood on darkness, clinging to a stone,
I saw the two leaping alive on ice,
On earth, on leaf, humus and withered vine:
The rabbit splendid in a shroud of shade,
The dog carved on the sunlight, on the air,
Fierce and magnificent his rippled hair,
The cockleburs shaking around his head.
Then, suddenly, the hare leaped beyond pain
Out of the open meadow, and the hound
Followed the voiceless dancer to the moon,
To dark, to death, to other meadows where
Singing young women dance around a fire,
Where love reveres the living.

                            I alone
Scatter this hulk about the dampened ground;
And while the moon rises beyond me, throw
The ribs and spine out of their perfect shape.
For a last charm to the dead, I lift the skull
And toss it over the maples like a ball.
Strewn to the woods, now may that spirit sleep
That flamed over the ground a year ago.
I know the mole will heave a shinbone over,
The earthworm snuggle for a nap on paws,
The honest bees build honey in the head;
The earth knows how to handle the great dead
Who lived the body out, and broke its laws,
Knocked down a fence, tore up a field of clover.

Three Steps to the Graveyard

When I went there first,
In the spring, it was evening,
It was long hollow thorn
Laid under the locust,
And near to my feet
The crowfoot, the mayapple
Trod their limbs down
Till the stalk blew over.
It grew summer, O riches
Of girls on the lawn,
And boys' locks lying
Tousled on knees,
The picknickers leaving,
The day gone down.

When I went there again,
I walked with my father
Who held in his hand
The crowfoot, the mayapple,
And under my hands,
To hold off the sunlight,
I saw him going,
Between two trees;
When the lawn lay empty
It was the year's end,
It was the darkness,

It was long hollow thorn
To wound the bare shade,
The sheaf and the blade.

O now as I go there
The crowfoot, the mayapple
Blear the gray pond;
Beside the still waters
The field mouse tiptoes,
To hear the air sounding
The long hollow thorn.
I lean to the hollow,
But nothing blows there,
The day goes down.
The field mice flutter
Like grass and are gone,
And a skinny old woman
Scrubs at a stone,
Between two trees.

Father

In paradise I poised my foot above the boat and said:
Who prayed for me?
                              But only the dip of an oar
In water sounded; slowly fog from some cold shore
Circled in wreaths around my head.

But who is waiting?
                              And the wind began,
Transfiguring my face from nothingness
To tiny weeping eyes. And when my voice
Grew real, there was a place
Far, far below on earth. There was a tiny man—

It was my father wandering round the waters at the wharf.
Irritably he circled and he called
Out to the marine currents up and down,
But heard only a cold unmeaning cough,
And saw the oarsman in the mist enshawled.

He drew me from the boat. I was asleep.
And we went home together.

Elegy in a Firelit Room

The window showed a willow in the west,
But windy dry. No folly weeping there.
A sparrow hung a wire about its breast
And spun across the air.

Instead of paying winter any mind,
I ran my fingerprints across the glass,
To feel the crystal forest sown by wind,
And one small face:

A child among the frozen bushes lost,
Breaking the white and rigid twigs between
Fingers more heavenly than hands of dust,
And fingernails more clean.

Beyond, the willow would not cry for cold,
The sparrow hovered long enough to stare;
The face between me and the wintered world
Began to disappear;

Because some friendly hands behind my back
Fumbled the coal and tended up the fire.
Warmth of the room waved to the window sash,
The face among the forest fell to air.

The glass began to weep instead of eyes,
A slow gray feather floated down the sky.
Delicate bone, finger and bush, and eyes
Yearned to the kissing fire and fell away.

Over the naked pasture and beyond,
A frozen bird lay down among the dead
Weeds, and the willow strode upon the wind
And would not bow its head.

Arrangements with Earth for Three Dead Friends

Sweet earth, he ran and changed his shoes to go
Outside with other children through the fields.
He panted up the hills and swung from trees
Wild as a beast but for the human laughter
That tumbled like a cider down his cheeks.
Sweet earth, the summer has been gone for weeks,
And weary fish already sleeping under water
Below the banks where early acorns freeze.
Receive his flesh and keep it cured of colds.
Button his coat and scarf his throat from snow.

And now, bright earth, this other is out of place
In what, awake, we speak about as tombs.
He sang in houses when the birds were still
And friends of his were huddled round till dawn
After the many nights to hear him sing.
Bright earth, his friends remember how he sang
Voices of night away when wind was one.
Lonely the neighborhood beneath your hill
Where he is waved away through silent rooms.
Listen for music, earth, and human ways.

Dark earth, there is another gone away,
But she was not inclined to beg of you
Relief from water falling or the storm.
She was aware of scavengers in holes

Of stone, she knew the loosened stones that fell
Indifferently as pebbles plunging down a well
And broke for the sake of nothing human souls.
Earth, hide your face from her where dark is warm.
She does not beg for anything, who knew
The change of tone, the human hope gone gray.

Lament for My Brother on a Hayrake

Cool with the touch of autumn, waters break
Out of the pump at dawn to clear my eyes;
I leave the house, to face the sacrifice
Of hay, the drag and death. By day, by moon,
I have seen my younger brother wipe his face
And heave his arm on steel. He need not pass
Under the blade to waste his life and break;

The hunching of the body is enough
To violate his bones. That bright machine
Strips the revolving earth of more than grass;
Powered by the fire of summer, bundles fall
Folded to die beside a burlap shroud;
And so my broken brother may lie mown
Out of the wasted fallows, winds return,
Corn-yellow tassels of his hair blow down,
The summer bear him sideways in a bale
Of darkness to October's mow of cloud.

She Hid in the Trees from the Nurses

She stands between the trees and holds
One hand in the other, still.
Now far away the evening folds
Around the siloes and the hill.

She sees, slowly, the gardener
Return to check the gate before
The smoke begins to soften the air
And June bugs try the open door.

And through the windows, washing hands,
The patients have the mattress made,
Their trousers felt for colored stones,
The pleasures of the noon recalled:

For some were caught and held for hours
By spiders skating over a pond,
Some parted veils of hollyhocks
And looked for rabbit holes beyond.

But now the trousers lie in rows,
She sees the undressed shadows creep
Through half-illuminated minds
And chase the hare and flower to sleep.

She too must answer summons now,
And play the chimes inside her brain
When whistles of attendants blow;
Yet, for a while, she would remain,

And dabble her feet in the damp grass,
And lean against a yielding stalk,
And spread her name in dew across
The pebbles where the droplets walk.

Minutes away a nurse will come
Across the lawn and call for her;
The starlight calls the robin home,
The swans retire beneath their wings.

Surely her mind is clear enough
To hear her name among the trees.
She must remember home and love
And skirts that sway below her knees.

But why must she desert the shade
And sleep between the walls all night?
Why must a lonely girl run mad
To gain the simple, pure delight

Of staying, when the others leave,
To write a name or hold a stone?
Of hearing bobwhites flute their love
Though buildings loudly tumble down?

 TO TROUBLED FRIENDS

To a Defeated Saviour

Do you forget the shifting hole
Where the slow swimmer fell aground
And floundered for your fishing pole
Above the snarl of string and sound?
You never seem to turn your face
Directly toward the river side,
Or up the bridge, or anyplace
Near where the skinny swimmer died.

You stand all day and look at girls,
Or climb a tree, or change a tire;
But I have seen the colored swirls
Of water flow to livid fire
Across your sleeping nose and jaws,
Transfiguring both the bone and skin
To muddy banks and sliding shoals
You and the drowned kid tumble in.

You see his face, upturning, float
And bob across your wavering bed;
His wailing fingers call your boat,
His voice throws up the ruddy silt,
The bleary vision prays for light
In sky behind your frozen hands;
But sinking in the dark all night,
You charm the shore with bloomless wands.

The circling tow, the shadowy pool
Shift underneath us everywhere.
You would have raised him, flesh and soul,
Had you been strong enough to dare;
You would have lifted him to breathe,
Believing your good hands would keep
His body clear of your own death:
This dream, this drowning in your sleep.

To a Troubled Friend

Weep, and weep long, but do not weep for me,
Nor, long lamenting, raise, for any word
Of mine that beats above you like a bird,
Your voice, or hand. But shaken clear, and free,
Be the bare maple, bough where nests are made
Snug in the season's wrinkled cloth of frost;
Be leaf, by hardwood knots, by tendrils crossed
On tendrils, stripped, uncaring; give no shade.

Give winter nothing; hold; and let the flake
Poise or dissolve along your upheld arms.
All flawless hexagons may melt and break;
While you must feel the summer's rage of fire,
Beyond this frigid season's empty storms,
Banished to bloom, and bear the birds' desire.

Poem for Kathleen Ferrier

1

I leaned to hear your song,
The breathing and the echo;
And when it dropped away,
I thought, for one deaf moment,
That I could never listen
To any other voice.

2

But the land is deep in sound.
The sleepy hares and crickets
Remember how to cry.
The birds have not forgotten
(The tanager, the sparrow)
The tumbled, rising tone.

3

The sounds go on, and on,
In spite of what the morning
Or evening dark has done.
We have no holy voices
Like yours to lift above us,
Yet we cannot be still.

4

All earth is loud enough.
Then why should I be sorry
(The owl scritches alive)
To stand before a shadow,
And see a cold piano
Half hidden by a drape?

5

No reason I can give.
Uttering tongues are busy,
Mount the diminished air
(The breathing and the echo)
Enough to keep the ear
Half satisfied forever.

A Song for the Middle of the Night

By way of explaining to my son the following curse by
Eustace Deschamps: "Happy is he who has no children;
for babies bring nothing but crying and stench."

Now first of all he means the night
    You beat the crib and cried
And brought me spinning out of bed
    To powder your backside.
I rolled your buttocks over
    And I could not complain:
Legs up, la la, legs down, la la,
    Back to sleep again.

Now second of all he means the day
    You dabbled out of doors
And dragged a dead cat Billy-be-damned
    Across the kitchen floors.
I rolled your buttocks over
    And made you sing for pain:
Legs up, la la, legs down, la la,
    Back to sleep again.

But third of all my father once
    Laid me across his knee
And solved the trouble when he beat
    The yowling out of me.
He rocked me on his shoulder
    When razor straps were vain:
Legs up, la la, legs down, la la,
    Back to sleep again.

So roll upon your belly, boy,
    And bother being cursed.
You turn the household upside down,
    But you are not the first.
Deschamps the poet blubbered too,
    For all his fool disdain:
Legs up, la la, legs down, la la,
    Back to sleep again.

A Presentation of Two Birds to My Son

Chicken. How shall I tell you what it is,
And why it does not float with tanagers?
Its ecstasy is dead, it does not care.
Its children huddle underneath its wings,
And altogether lounge against the shack,
Warm in the slick tarpaulin, smug and soft.

You must not fumble in your mind
The genuine ecstasy of climbing birds
With that dull fowl.
When your grandfather held it by the feet
And laid the skinny neck across
The ragged chopping block,
The flop of wings, the jerk of the red comb
Were a dumb agony,
Stupid and meaningless. It was no joy
To leave the body beaten underfoot;
Life was a flick of corn, a steady roost.
Chicken. The sound is plain.

Look up and see the swift above the trees.
How shall I tell you why he always veers
And banks around the shaken sleeve of air,
Away from ground? He hardly flies on brains;
Pockets of air impale his hollow bones.
He leans against the rainfall or the sun.

You must not mix this pair of birds
Together in your mind before you know
That both are clods.
What makes the chimney swift approach the sky
Is ecstasy, a kind of fire
That beats the bones apart
And lets the fragile feathers close with air.
Flight too is agony,
Stupid and meaningless. Why should it be joy
To leave the body beaten underfoot,
To mold the limbs against the wind, and join
Those clean dark glides of Dionysian birds?
The flight is deeper than your father, boy.

To a Hostess Saying Good Night

Shake out the ruffle, turn and go,
Over the trellis blow the kiss.
Some of the guests will never know
Another night to shadow this.
Some of the birds awake in vines
Will never see another face
So frail, so lovely anyplace
Between the birdbath and the bines.

O dark come never down to you.
I look away and look away:
Over the moon the shadows go,
Over your shoulder, nebulae.
Some of the vast, the vacant stars
Will never see your face at all,
Your frail, your lovely eyelids fall
Between Andromeda and Mars.

A Poem about George Doty
in the Death House

Lured by the wall, and drawn
To stare below the roof,
Where pigeons nest aloof
From prowling cats and men,
I count the sash and bar
Secured to granite stone,
And note the daylight gone,
Supper and silence near.

Close to the wall inside,
Immured, empty of love,
A man I have wondered of
Lies patient, vacant-eyed.
A month and a day ago
He stopped his car and found
A girl on the darkening ground,
And killed her in the snow.

Beside his cell, I am told,
Hardy perennial bums
Complain till twilight comes
For hunger and for cold.
They hardly know of a day
That saw their hunger pass.
Bred to the dark, their flesh
Peacefully withers away.

The man who sits alone,
He is the one for wonder,
Who sways his fingers under
The cleanly shaven chin,
Who sees, in the shaving mirror
Pinned to the barren wall,
The uprooted ghost of all:
The simple, easy terror.

Caught between sky and earth,
Poor stupid animal,
Stripped naked to the wall,
He saw the blundered birth
Of daemons beyond sound.
Sick of the dark, he rose
For love, and now he goes
Back to the broken ground.

Now, as he grips the chain
And holds the wall, to bear
What no man ever bore,
He hears the bums complain;
But I mourn no soul but his,
Not even the bums who die,
Nor the homely girl whose cry
Crumbled his pleading kiss.

To a Fugitive

The night you got away, I dreamed you rose
Out of the earth to lean on a young tree.
Then they were there, hulking the moon away,
The great dogs rooting, snuffing up the grass.
You raise a hand, hungry to hold your lips
Out of the wailing air; but lights begin
Spidering the ground; oh they come closing in,
The beam searches your face like fingertips.

Hurry, Maguire, hammer the body down,
Crouch to the wall again, shackle the cold
Machine guns and the sheriff and the cars:
Divide the bright bars of the cornered bone,
Strip, run for it, break the last law, unfold,
Dart down the alley, race between the stars.

III LOVES

Eleutheria

Rubbing her mouth along my mouth she lost
Illusions of the sky, the dreams it offered:
The pale cloud walking home to winter, dust
Blown to a shell of sails so far above
That autumn landscape where we lay and suffered
The fruits of summer in the fields of love.

We lay and heard the apples fall for hours,
The stripping twilight plundered trees of boughs,
The land dissolved beneath the rabbit's heels,
And far away I heard a window close,
A haying wagon heave and catch its wheels,
Some water slide and stumble and be still.
The dark began to climb the empty hill.

If dark Eleutheria turned and lay
Forever beside me, who would care for years?
The throat, the supple belly, the warm thigh
Burgeoned against the earth; I lay afraid,
For who could bear such beauty under the sky?
I would have held her loveliness in air,
Away from things that lured me to decay:
The ground's deliberate riches, fallen pears,
Bewildered apples blown to mounds of shade.

Lovers' location is the first to fade.
They wander back in winter, but there is
No comfortable grass to couch a dress.
Musicians of the yellow weeds are dead.
And she, remembering something, turns to hear
Either a milkweed float or a thistle fall.
Bodiless shadow thrown along a wall,
She glides lightly; the pale year follows her.

The moments ride away, the locust flute
Is silvered thin and lost, over and over.
She will return some evening to discover
The tree uplifted to the very root,
The leaves shouldered away, with lichen grown
Among the interlacings of the stone,
October blowing dust, and summer gone
Into a dark barn, like a hiding lover.

Autumnal

Soft, where the shadow glides,
The yellow pears fell down.
The long bough slowly rides
The air of my delight.

Air, though but nothing, air
Falls heavy down your shoulder.
You hold in burdened hair
The color of my delight.

Neither the hollow pear,
Nor leaf among the grass,
Nor wind that wails the year
Against your leaning ear,
Will alter my delight:

That holds the pear upright
And sings along the bough,
Warms to the mellow sun.
The song of my delight
Gathers about you now,
Is whispered through, and gone.

The Ungathered Apples

I saw between a shadow and a bough
Two apples swinging. I was still beneath.
The nippled tips are dry and empty now,
And dry the earth.

But I was still alive, and offered hands
To stir the perfect balance of the pair,
Fumble and turn the blouse of woven leaves,
Lift the rose skin to air.

I laid my knee against a kneeling root,
Allowed a lower bough to hold my back,
And heard the limb beneath the quivering fruit
Sicken and crack.

Shamed for the clumsiness of my clambering bones,
Flung outward to the ground,
I lay and felt the judgment of the stones
Point without sound,

And saw, near heaven, globular and cold,
Depending on the bough I lay beneath,
The shadow of the ruddy and the gold
Bosoms that milked the earth.

And yet I held no anger. The slight lung
Of leaves went swelling round the globes,
Softly as though a naked woman sang
The ceremony of the fallen robes.

Surrendering, I lifted overhead
My quiet hands in hopeless prayer
For all the gathered apples of the dead
Hidden in cellars when the boughs are bare.

The Shadow and the Real

There was no more than shadow where
She leaned outside the kitchen door,
Stood in the sun and let her hair
Loosely float in the air and fall.
She tossed her body's form before
Her feet, and laid it down the wall.
And how was I to feel, therefore,
Shadow no more than darker air?

I rose, and crossed the room, to find
Her hands, her body, her green dress;
But where she stood, the sun behind
Demolished her from touch and sight.
Her body burned to emptiness,
Her hair caught summer in the light;
I sought, bewildered, for her face,
No more than splendid air, gone blind.

Witches Waken the Natural World in Spring

Warm in the underbough of dark
Willows is where the women go
To whisper how the barren park
Will shiver into blossom now.
It does not matter they are slim
Or plump as melons left too long
Upon the vine; beneath the dim
Spell of the willow they are strong.

And very seldom I remember
What revelations they have spoken.
I know I saw a willow tremble
In starlight once, a burdock broken,
Shaken by the voice of my girl
Who waved to heaven overhead;
And though she made a leaflet fall
I have forgotten what she said:

Except that spring was coming on
Or might have come already while
We lay beside a smooth-veined stone;
Except an owl sang half a mile
Away; except a starling's feather
Softened my face beside a root:
But how should I remember whether
She was the one who spoke, or not?

Morning Hymn to a Dark Girl

Summoned to desolation by the dawn,
I climb the bridge over the water, see
The Negro mount the driver's cabin and wave
Goodbye to the glum cop across the canal,
Goodbye to the flat face and empty eyes
Made human one more time. That uniform
Shivers and dulls against the pier, is stone.

Now in the upper world, the buses drift
Over the bridge, the gulls collect and fly,
Blown by the rush of rose; aseptic girls
Powder their lank deliberate faces, mount
The fog under the billboards. Over the lake
The windows of the rich waken and yawn.
Light blows across the city, dune on dune.

Caught by the scruff of the neck, and thrown out here
To the pale town, to the stone, to burial,
I celebrate you, Betty, flank and breast
Rich to the yellow silk of bed and floors;
Now half awake, your body blossoming trees;
One arm beneath your neck, your legs uprisen,
You blow dark thighs back, back into the dark.

Your shivering ankles skate the scented air;
Betty, burgeoning your golden skin, you poise
Tracing gazelles and tigers on your breasts,
Deep in the jungle of your bed you drowse;

Fine muscles of the rippling panthers move
And snuggle at your calves; under your arms
Mangoes and melons yearn; and glittering slowly,
Quick parakeets trill in your heavy trees,
O everywhere, Betty, between your boughs.

Pity the rising dead who fear the dark.
Soft Betty, locked from snickers in a dark
Brothel, dream on; scatter the yellow corn
Into the wilderness, and sleep all day.
For the leopards leap into the open grass,
Bananas, lemons fling air, fling odor, fall.
And, gracing darkly the dark light, you flow
Out of the grove to laugh at dreamy boys,
You greet the river with a song so low
No lover on a boat can hear, you slide
Silkily to the water, where you rinse
Your fluted body, fearless; though alive
Orangutans sway from the leaves and gaze,
Crocodiles doze along the oozy shore.

The Quail

Lost in the brush, bound by the other path
To find the house,
You let me know how many voices,
How many shifting bodies you possessed,
How you could flit away to follow birds,
And yet be near.

A quail implored the hollow for a home,
A covey of dark to lie in under stars;
And, when it sang, you left my hand
To voyage how softly down the even grass
And see the meadow where the quails lie down,
Flushed in the dark by hunters' broken guns.

You left my side before I knew the way
To find the house,
And soon you called across the hollow
To say you were alive and still on earth;
And, when you sang, the quail began to cry,
So I lost both.

The blue dusk bore feathers beyond our eyes,
Dissolved all wings as you, your hair dissolved,
Your frame of bone blown hollow as a house
Beside the path, were borne away from me
Farther than birds for whom I did not care,
Comingled with the dark complaining air.

I could have called the simple dark to fade,
To find the house,
And left you standing silent;
But stained away by maple leaves, and led
From tree to tree by wands of luring ghosts,
You knew my love,

You knew my feet would never turn away
From any forest where your body was,
Though vanished up the disembodied dark.
And when I found you laughing under trees,
The quail began to trill and flute away,
As far away as hands that reach for hands;
But, when it sang, you kissed me out of sound.

IV STORIES AND VOICES

to Elizabeth Willerton

Three Speeches in a Sick Room

1. The Wife to the Husband

Before you sit and mourn my awkward death,
I know how many tales I ought to tell,
Of how I've prayed to meet in heaven
You and your mother.

And so all afternoon I've tried to turn
My mind away from the warm smell of sun,
And the fat fields of earth
Where girls lie down.

I cannot turn my face away from light,
I lean across the pillow, breathe
The whole outside of odor till I cough,
And fall back, still.
You and your mother and geraniums
Strewing me over!
Smell of the dead flower fills me,
Prayers rear up in my throat,
But cannot breach
The wall of flower and sun outside on earth;
They paw and plunge
Back in my body, down,
Down, to bone again.

Come closer. I can't see. You hang in fuzz
Like a beautiful bug in webs
I've dragged down many a time,
The dust of the house.
No. That's too close. Sit down.

You listen now, the door is opening wide,
And now annihilated by the dark,
I have to speak.
It does no good to bellow; listen close.

I had a dream.
I met you near the house cutting the grass,
And touched your arm.
I would have stayed, but you were scaly, cold,
And turned upon me, flickering your tongue,
And smiling with your mouth but not your eyes.
I ran away, though far away behind
You searched and lashed the grass.

The woods grew thick with briars,
Oh lovely slashes
That made me feel my song!
The gully where I went was sick with flowers,
Sweet little bells I broke in bits
To suck the honey out of the heart
And beat the racing bees.

I stood beneath the locust bough
And dragged the bells of bloom
Out of the way, out of the way!
Can't you see?

The thorn cut my hands, but I held.
I wasn't hunting blossoms in the woods,
Or the sweet hum of bees.
The honey ran all over my hands,
When I reached through and scared some birds away—

It was the stars, the beating stars, I sought,
Flickering in dark.
Hurried, I dragged my body under the limb,
And broke it down—

Too simple there, too desolately clear
To touch with hands,
They glittered white as bones,
Too desolately clear.

I found the path again, but halfway down
The earth dissolved away, I seemed to go
Where nothing lay but air.
My arms and hands burned with the broken flowers
And the green thorns.
And I met a man who loved me
Back in the drying shade.

He wasn't you. He wasn't you. He died
In my long arms. Be still, it was a dream,
A fever dream. And I am waking now.
Why is it dark, is that the sun again?
It gets so late.
Why must you hang there in the darkening web?
Go now, go now.

2. The Husband to the Doctor

I didn't do a thing to her.
Why did she have to die?
Before you sit and mourn her awkward death,
Sit down with me.

I know you understand me when I say
I wish you'd keep it still.
Nobody has to know she rolled and wailed
And gibbered like a cat across the bed
And waved me out.

What happened there?
Sometimes she seemed as silly as a child,
And I could lead her then;
It was so easy, every word she spoke
Was plain and clear:
She asked me out to walk and take the air
Along the river, down the railroad track
To look for plantain greens,
She held my hand,
She pointed out the color of the rain,
She liked the sky,
She even let me cry against her arm
For the dead child—

But suddenly the stars, she cried about the stars.
I couldn't follow her.
Why should she curse me out because I lost her?
I don't know how!
I never asked for anything but her,
And I was there with her. God! I was there.

Doctor, you've sat before
By the beds of crying women,
You seem to know the rest
Of what goes on when blankets are thrown off:
Give me the word!

Oh, everybody's death's a festering pain;
All I can do is pray my bones to hold.
She died in a warm bed, by God,
And I was there.
She knows I loved,
She knows I tried to follow where she flew,
I know I wasn't there when she went singing
To shadows after dark.
And now she's gone again, and I can follow
Until I die, but I don't understand.

   3. The Doctor to the Wife

Dear love, say nothing now,
Say nothing ever again.
I will sit down beside you,
Remove the burning cover
That never again will burn;

And turn the pillow away
So I can see your face,
Your long and quiet lashes
Laid to your cheek in silence;
And listen for your voice:

Knowing that song no more
Will beat inside your breast,

Knowing it is no use now
To tell you aloud I love you
Beyond the hope of love.

You must not stand in hell
And hate his stupid face,
You must not beg the powers
To chain him high in heaven
While you lie damned and free.

He never learned your pain,
But let him bear his own,
And let him hunt his shadow
Of folly or mud or music.
Love, we are not the same.

So let his body be,
As he let be your own.
It is no use to lie there
In hell, and waste forever
On a thin, empty name.

You never cried at all,
You held the stony face.
Weep, love, now, in the shadow,
And I will lift the cover
Across your quiet eyes.

Dear love, be for the ground,
Say nothing ever again.
I loved you all for nothing
Except the word not spoken,
Except the name of love.

Sappho

*Ach, in den Armen hab ich sie alle verloren, du nur, du wirst immer wieder
geboren. . . .*   RILKE, *Die Aufzeichnungen des Malte Laurids Brigge*

The twilight falls; I soften the dusting feathers,
And clean again.
The house has lain and moldered for three days,
The windows smeared with rain, the curtains torn,
The mice come in,
The kitchen blown with cold.

I keep the house, and say no words.

It is true I am as twisted as the cactus
That gnarls and turns beside the milky light,
That cuts the fingers easily and means nothing,
For all the pain that shoots along the hand.
I dust the feathers down the yellow thorns,
I light the stove.

The gas curls round the iron fretwork, the flame
Floats above the lace,
And bounces like a dancer stayed on air.
Fire does not rest on iron, it drifts like a blue blossom
And catches on my breath;
Coiling, spinning, the blue foam of the gas fire
Writhes like a naked girl;
Turns up its face, like her.

She came to me in rain.
I did not know her, I did not know my name
After she left to bed her children down,

To phone her husband they were gone asleep,
And she, lying, a pure fire, in the feathers,
Dancing above the ironwork of her bed,
Roaring, and singeing nothing.
She had not wound her arms about me then,
She had not dared.
I only took her coat, and smiled to hear
How she had left her purse and her umbrella
In the theater, how she was sopping cold
With the fall rain; and mine was the one light
In the neighborhood. She came to my gas fire
And lay before it, sprawled, her pure bare shoulders
Folded in a doze, a clear, cold curve of stone.

I only leaned above the hair,
Turned back the quilt, arranged the feet, the arms,
And kissed the sleeping shoulder, lightly, like the rain;
And when she woke to wear her weathered clothes,
I sent her home.
She floated, a blue blossom, over the street.

And when she came again,
It was not long before she turned to me,
And let her shawl slide down her neck and shoulder,
Let her hair fall.
And when she came again,
It did not rain.

Her husband came to pluck her like an apple,
As the drunken farmer lurches against the tree,
Grips the green globe not long beyond its bloom,

And tears the skin, brutally, out of the bark,
Leaves the whole bough broken,
The orchard torn with many footprints,
The fence swung wide
On a raw hinge.

And now it is said of me
That my love is nothing because I have borne no children,
Or because I have fathered none;
That I twisted the twig in my hands
And cut the blossom free too soon from the seed;
That I lay across the fire,
And snuffed it dead sooner than draft or rain.

But I have turned away, and drawn myself
Upright to walk along the room alone.
Across the dark the spines of cactus plants
Remind me how I go—aloof, obscure,
Indifferent to the words the children chalk
Against my house and down the garden walls.
They cannot tear the garden out of me,
Nor smear my love with names. Love is a cliff,
A clear, cold curve of stone, mottled by stars,
Smirched by the morning, carved by the dark sea
Till stars and dawn and waves can slash no more,
Till the rock's heart is found and shaped again.

I keep the house and say no words, the evening
Falls like a petal down the shawl of trees.
I light the fire and see the blossom dance
On air alone; I will not douse that flame,

That searing flower; I will burn in it.
I will not banish love to empty rain.

For I know that I am asked to hate myself
For their sweet sake
Who sow the world with child.
I am given to burn on the dark fire they make
With their sly voices.

But I have burned already down to bone.
There is a fire that burns beyond the names
Of sludge and filth of which this world is made.
Agony sears the dark flesh of the body,
And lifts me higher than the smoke, to rise
Above the earth, above the sacrifice;
Until my soul flares outward like a blue
Blossom of gas fire dancing in mid-air:
Free of the body's work of twisted iron.

A Gesture by a Lady with an Assumed Name

Letters she left to clutter up the desk
Burned in the general gutter when the maid
Came in to do the room and take the risk
Of slipping off the necklace round her head.

Laundry she left to clutter up the floor
Hung to rachitic skeletons of girls
Who worked the bars or labored up the stair
To crown her blowsy ribbons on their curls.

Lovers she left to clutter up the town
Mourned in the chilly morgue and went away,
All but the husbands sneaking up and down
The stairs of that apartment house all day.

What were they looking for? The cold pretense
Of lamentation offered in a stew?
A note? A gift? A shred of evidence
To love when there was nothing else to do?

Or did they rise to weep for that unheard-
Of love, whose misery cries and does not care
Whether or not the madam hears a word
Or skinny children watch the trodden stair?

Whether or not, how could she love so many,
Then turn away to die as though for none?
I saw the last offer a child a penny
To creep outside and see the cops were gone.

Mutterings over the Crib of a Deaf Child

"How will he hear the bell at school
Arrange the broken afternoon,
And know to run across the cool
Grasses where the starlings cry,
Or understand the day is gone?"

Well, someone lifting curious brows
Will take the measure of the clock.
And he will see the birchen boughs
Outside sagging dark from the sky,
And the shade crawling upon the rock.

"And how will he know to rise at morning?
His mother has other sons to waken,
She has the stove she must build to burning
Before the coals of the nighttime die;
And he never stirs when he is shaken."

I take it the air affects the skin,
And you remember, when you were young,
Sometimes you could feel the dawn begin,
And the fire would call you, by and by,
Out of the bed and bring you along.

"Well, good enough. To serve his needs
All kinds of arrangements can be made.
But what will you do if his finger bleeds?

Or a bobwhite whistles invisibly
And flutes like an angel off in the shade?"

He will learn pain. And, as for the bird,
It is always darkening when that comes out.
I will putter as though I had not heard,
And lift him into my arms and sing
Whether he hears my song or not.

Crucifixion on Thursday

We howled for crumbs under the flickered tapers,
Tapped at a stone; but no one came to lean
Against the gate or soften the great hinges
At the sharp cry of toes in the dank courtyard.

New at the game, I waited long for the others
To look me over and teach me the soft songs
They made over the cups on the stone corners;
No voice advised me, no hands moved.

Surely, after the lash of whips to our shoulders
We bore together before the governor's house,
After the groans we gave in the dust together,
They could have taught me songs, the begging gesture,

The face to make at soldiers, the sly cringe
A flash before the blow falls, to escape it.
But I learned nothing of art from these serpents,
The halt and limping, frigid in their own sorrow.

Sick, then, of whining folly in the world,
Whether it be the ache of recent wounds
Or sneaking artifice to clutch for coins,
I turned them in—scuffled by night away

While they were stealing apples off a wall
And a warm loaf of bread, a skin of wine
To nourish the belly under the dark stars;
They cast me out—I walked to the judge upright,

Clamored for justice, cursed all men who beg
Under the false hunger; and took my money
To jingle under their crosses on the hill,
To mock them with a bauble of bitten silver;

And saw their bones reach out beneath the skin
Stained like a sow's backbone; and knew their voices
Who taught me nothing more than names of streets
Or a low snatch of tune I could not use.

Now the great soldiers leave their nervous horses,
And drag the beggars down from heaven.
The ditches will be full of mouths tonight
But no sound of their music nor of anguish;

And sky be clear in starlight, earth be clear
Of horses, beggars, women. So I walk homeward,
Sneaking again to miss the prowl of troops:
The streets are ordered clear tonight by twelve.

And no one knows who gave away the names
Of those dead on the hill, so I am safe,
Even against myself. For I care nothing;
The dead fall down in pain before and after.

What comes tomorrow, what fell yesterday
May never raise the dead, so low they lie;
Echoes of hoofbeats deafen the dim city,
Thieves scuffle in dark, and pain continues.

The Angel

Last night, before I came to bear
The clean edge of my wing upon the boulder,
I walked about the town.
The people seemed at peace that he was dead:
A beggar carried water out of a door,
And young men gathered round the corner
To spell the night.

I walked, like a folded bird, about the towers
And sang softly to the blue levels of evening,
I slid down treeless, featherless, bemused:
At curious faces whispering round a fire
And sniffing chestnuts sugared by a woman;
At a vague child heaving a beetle over
In dust, to see it swimming on its back.

Under an arch I found a woman lean
Weeping for loneliness: away from her
A young man whistle toward the crowds;
Out of an open window pigeons flew
And a slow dove fluted for nothing—the girl
Blew to the air a melody lost on me.

Laid in a pile of stone, how could he weep
For that calm town?
Looped in a yoke of darkened garden,
He murmured blood out of his heart for love,
Hallowed a soldier, took the savage kiss
And gave it back a warm caress;

Yet no one changed.

Tossing aside the worry of the place,
As someone threw an apple core across
A wall I walked beside, I sought delight
Pebble by pebble, song by song, and light
By light, singly, among the river boats.
Down to the river at the end I came.

But then a girl appeared, to wash her hair.
Struck stupid by her face,
I stood there, sick to love her, sick of sky.
The child, the beetle, chestnut fires, the song
Of girl and dove
Shuddered along my wings and arms.
She slipped her bodice off, and a last wave
Of shadow oiled her shoulder till it shone;
Lifting her arms to loosen the soft braids
She looked across the water. I looked down
And felt my wings waving aside the air,
Furious to fly. For I could never bear
Belly and breast and thigh against the ground.

Now, having heaved the hidden hollow open
As I was sent to do, seen Jesus waken
And guided the women there, I wait to rise.
To feel a weapon gouge between the ribs,
He hung with a shut mouth:
For curious faces round a chestnut fire,
For the slow fluting doves
Lost on a trellis, for the laughing girl
Who frightened me away.

But now I fumble at the single joy
Of dawn. On the pale ruffle of the lake
The ripples weave a color I can bear.
Under a hill I see the city sleep
And fade. The perfect pleasure of the eyes:
A tiny bird bathed in a bowl of air,
Carving a yellow ripple down the bines,
Posing no storm to blow my wings aside
As I drift upward dropping a white feather.

The Assignation

After the winter thawed away, I rose,
Remembering what you said. Below the field
Where I was dead, the crinkled leaf and blade
Summoned my body, told me I must go.
Across the road I saw some other dead
Revive their little fires, and bow the head
To someone still alive and long ago.
Low in the haze a pall of smoke arose.

Inside the moon's hollow is a hale gray man
Who washed his hands, and waved me where to go:
Up the long hill, the mound of lunar snow,
Around three lapping pebbles, over the crossed
Arms of an owl nailed to the southern sky.
I spun three times about, I scattered high,
Over my shoulder, clouds of salt and dust.
The earth began to clear. I saw a man.

He said the sun was falling toward the trees,
The picnic nearly over. Small on the lake
The sails were luring lightning out of dark,
While quieter people guided slim canoes.
I hid in bushes, shy. Already cars
Shuttled away, the earliest evening stars
Blurred in a cloud. A lone child left his shoes
Half in the sand, and slept beneath the trees.

With fires demolished, everybody gone
To root in bushes, congregate by trees
Or haul the yellow windows down to haze,
I lost my way. Water in water fell,
The badgers nibbled rootlets up the shore,
For dancing more than food, where long before
Women had gossiped. Chanting a soft farewell,
Canaries swung. Then everything was gone.

No hurry for me there, I let my dress
Fall to the lawn, the pleasure of the silk
Wind with the subtle grass, berries and milk
Of skin sweeten me. Snuggling, I lay prone,
Barren yet motherly for what might come
Out of the emptied branches, man or flame.
I shivered slightly. Everything was gone,
Everyone gone. I kicked aside my dress.

O then it was you I waited for, to hold
The soft leaves of my bones between your hands
And warm them back to life, to fashion wands
Out of my shining arms. O it was you
I loved before my dying and long after,
You, you I could not find. The air fell softer,
My snatch of breath gave out, but no one blew
My name in hallowed weeds. Lonely to hold

Some hand upon me, lest it float away
And be as dead as I, thrown in a sack
Of air to drown in air, I rose, lay back
In trees, and died again. The spiders care

For trellises they hold against the sky,
Except for walls of air the houses die
And fall; and only for my flesh of air
Your flesh of earth would lean and drift away;

But you cared nothing, living, false to me.
What could I do but take a daemon then
And slouch about in dust, eager for pain
Or anything, to keep your memory clear?
A thing came down from the dark air on wings
And rummaged at my limbs, to hold my wings
Down in the dirt; I could not see for fear.
The thing withdrew, full of the dark and me.

And I was riven. Even my poor ghost
Can never stand beside your window now;
I stir the wind, I chatter at a bough,
But make no sound. Your cowardice may keep
You from your assignation with my ghost,
The love you promised me when I was dust,
Not air. And yet I cannot even sleep,
I cannot die, but I will feel my ghost

Driven to find this orchard every year,
This picnic ground, and wait till everyone
Tires of the sundown, turns the headlights on,
To float them off like moths into the dark.
I will stand up to strip my hunger off,
And stare, and mumble, knowing all your love
Is cut beside my name on the white rock,
While you forget the promise and the year.

You sat beside the bed, you took my hands;
And when I lay beyond all speech, you said,
You swore to love me after I was dead,
To meet me in a grove and love me still,
Love the white air, the shadow where it lay.
Dear love, I called your name in air today,
I saw the picnic vanish down the hill,
And waved the moon awake, with empty hands.

Come Forth

Lazarus lay to see the body turn.
The femur first removed itself from arms,
The elbows folded under each other soon.

The clavicle and vertebrae and shin
Divided like the stars and let the air
Caress the flesh awake before it fell.

Only the torpid brain would not remove.
From far away beyond the granite walls
A vowel of longing tore the wind in two.

Come forth, it said. *But who is this who cried?*
For I have left the human long ago,
My flesh a synagogue the flame has eaten.

Before the voice the worms began to pray,
And fled away howling into the granite.
The shin returned to spring a leaping leg,

The skull rounded itself upon the brain,
The heart arose and cried with joy for pain,
The arteries assumed a thud again.

And the hair furied on the shocking head,
And muscles blossomed like the thunderhead
That trumpets the pale tropics to green storm.

The stones rolling away and the air thrust
Into the lung of the cave, Lazarus knew
The unholy and indifferent sting of wind

Across the flesh of man. Outside, the sun
Flayed the same bone as before. Nevertheless
His treading skeleton clattered like a choir

And waved him forward on a crest of praise.
A wall or two away the calling voice
Shook like a pacing father, and was still.

O blessed fire, O harsh and loving air.

Erinna to Sappho

I saw your shoulder swell and pitch
Alive, your fingers, curving, turn
To summon me above that ditch
    Where I lay down.

Yet as I came, you turned about
And waved to someone out of sight,
Someone you could not do without
    That very night.

Who was she? for I only saw
Mellifluous berries fall from vines,
Long apple blooms depress a bough,
    Clustering wines

Dripping their liquor as they hung
In spray and tendril, curling hair.
You flickered your inviting tongue
    At no one there;

No one but air, garden, the hewn
Poet above his pedestal,
Lyre in the marble, song in stone,
    The trees, the wall;

Unless there was, before I rose,
One of the hollow things who walk
The world in anguish, wearing clothes
    Just before dark;

And you were calling out to her
Or him, whatever bodiless
Presences hollow spirits bear
     Beneath their dress.

Whether I knew or did not know,
Under the misery of my skin,
What pale plunderer looted you
     Outside and in,

I leaped, above the ditch of earth,
Bodily, clung my arms around
Your poising knees, and brought us both
     Back to the ground,

Where we belong, if anywhere,
To hide in our own hollowed dust.
Whatever I gave, I gave no bare
     Pain of a ghost.

I offered, worshiping, that sweet
Cluster of liquors caught in globes,
I burst the riches till they wet
     Your tousled robes;

And though I stole from you no more
Than fireflies gain of the soft moon,
You turned to me, long, long before
     The ghost was gone,

If ghost it was, or melon rind,
Or stag's skeleton hung to dry,
Lover, or song, or only wind
     Sighing your sigh.

The Three Husbands

Don't let anyone tell you they were brave,
Or proud of feeding eight of us every day,
Or anything but men who know they have
Families a-building; little enough to say.

The last was taller than the other two,
And used to help the surgeon with the trees.
He sang each evening everything he knew
And knelt beside the cradle on his knees.
I hardly blame him doing such a thing;
Only the youngest child was his, you know.
Besides, he taught the oldest how to sing.
He passed away about twelve years ago.

The second was a carpenter, who tried,
One year, to build three sections at a time:
The roof and porch and cellar wall. He died
With hacking cough he caught without a coat.
I worked all night to keep him covered up
With mustard pack that ran away with sweat.
I fed him sassafras, and made him sleep—
I think he died at night, but I forget.

But that was quite a while ago, young man,
And mostly I remember his light voice
That used to wake me up, when I was gone
To sleep again, after the wracking noise
Of seven children stomping off to school.

There was some music, too, he used to make;
If you could stand the song of an old fool,
I'd try to sing it now, for someone's sake.

The first of all was stranger than the others,
And yet his face is clearest now; his hands
Took both of mine after we left his brothers
And walked five miles to see the pasture lands.
Sixty-five years ago we stood and heard
The wind slide down the hillside like a shawl,
And I still see a sparrow, a hungry bird,
Fly over his slim shoulder, fly and fall.
Oh, I can cock my ear and listen close
For every song I knew and every voice:
The last one sang all evening; he was tall;
The second one strong, the builder of this house.
But it was the first who saw the sparrow fall,
And laid his shaven face against my face.
Yet he never sang a song to me at all.
And he hardly said a word to me at all.

A Little Girl on Her Way to School

When the dark dawn humped off to die
The air sang, clearly the county bells
Rang in the light from trees to wells
And silkened every catbird cry.

Webbed in a gown of yellow-white,
Gauzed as a robin where the tree
Blows down over the eyelids, she
Limped on beyond me in the light.

One bell before I woke, the stones
Under the balls of her soft feet
Cried out to her, the leaves in the wet
All tumbled toward her name at once.

And while my waking hung in poise
Between the air and the damp earth,
I saw her startle to the breath
Of birds beginning in her voice.

Be careful of holes, the catbird said,
His nest hanging below her hair,
Nudging the robins windward there,
Whorling the air of glint and shade.

Fall in the hole, the pigeon swore,
His feathers beckoning her to ground,
Burling the sparrows out of sound,
Whorling the glints of shade and air.

Cling to the edge, cling to the edge,
Here, step lightly, touch my beak.
She listened, but she would not speak,
Following the white swan through the hedge.

A Call from the Front Porch

You love to sing of any name you know,
And I would follow to the witch of words
To spell your buried language in the air,
And understand. Yet every sign I read
Leads to the empty house, the dark garage.

Where do you go? The father's bafflement
Can scare out of your lips nothing but names
Of trees and gardens, lily, amaryllis
Floating into a tangle near the pond.
When I demand your way into the dark,
You flee my hand, my ceremonial hand.

Soon, as the sun laces the maple shade,
I stand in open doors, I call your name,
Knowing you hear no more of me than I
Hear of the gnome, the dragon, and the goat
Who whisper out of bushes, gesture, fold
Your arm around a rainspout under cloud,
Contriving a remembrancer of laughter.

The mystic lovers and the magic dead
People the garden; light, invisible
Determiners of seasons and men's pain
Snicker to you the tongue of troubled runes.
You love to speak of any song you know;
You led the kittens down the garden way
And saw them disappear, and saw them rise
Feathered to heaven, translated to the moon.

And one day rode your tricycle around
The dark garage, and hid for half an hour.
But when I followed, softly as I might,
To catch whatever daemon might be near,
Insect or bird, you looked above my head,
Smiled, nodded to a face of sunlight there.
Children around the corner chattered off,
I wiped your fingers with my handkerchief
And kissed your hair, tousled in summer dust.
Tracks of a cloven shadow led to trees.

Now, when I follow, tracks dissolve in space,
And only men running half mad can hear
A music playing; but soberly I arrive
To find you sitting innocent in grime.
I love to say your name, the name I know;
But cannot know what shadow stood with you,
What Nicken mocking my tall shadow down.
Go, wander then, hallow the earth awhile,
Loiter with birds or follow in the hedge
Wherever goat-feet lead from the dark house.
But come to me, boy, come to me once more
In twilight when the gardener rolls the hose
In circles up the lawn, and sprinklers fall
To nothing more than driplets under grass;
The porchlight coming on again, the voice
Serve to assure you of my searching hand:
Come to the kitchen now, and climb the stair.
I love the body, though the soul be gone
Picking about some brambles for an apple
Or dancing down a meadow with a gnome.

My Grandmother's Ghost

She skimmed the yellow water like a moth,
Trailing her feet across the shallow stream;
She saw the berries, paused and sampled them
Where a slight spider cleaned his narrow tooth.
Light in the air, she fluttered up the path,
So delicate to shun the leaves and damp,
Like some young wife, holding a slender lamp
To find her stray child, or the moon, or both.

Even before she reached the empty house,
She beat her wings ever so lightly, rose,
Followed a bee where apples blew like snow;
And then, forgetting what she wanted there,
Too full of blossom and green light to care,
She hurried to the ground, and slipped below.

THE YALE SERIES OF YOUNGER POETS, which is designed to provide a publishing medium for the first volumes of promising poets, is open to men and women under forty who have not previously had a book of verse published. W. H. Auden, the Editor of the Series, selects the winning volume in the annual contest and writes a preface for it. Manuscripts should be received before March 1 and should be addressed to the Editor, Yale Series of Younger Poets, Yale University Press, New Haven, Connecticut. Rules of the contest will be sent upon request.

VOLUMES ISSUED TO DATE

1. The Tempering. HOWARD BUCK
2. Forgotten Shrines. JOHN CHIPMAN FARRAR
3. Four Gardens. DAVID OSBORNE HAMILTON
4. Spires and Poplars. ALFRED RAYMOND BELLINGER
5. The White God and Other Poems. THOMAS CALDECOT CHUBB
6. Where Lilith Dances. DARL MACLEOD BOYLE
7. Wild Geese. THEODORE H. BANKS, JR.
8. Horizons. VIOLA C. WHITE
9. Wampum and Old Gold. HERVEY ALLEN
10. The Golden Darkness. OSCAR WILLIAMS
11. White April. HAROLD VINAL
12. Dreams and a Sword. MEDORA C. ADDISON
13. Hidden Waters. BERNARD RAYMUND
14. Attitudes. PAUL TANAQUIL
15. The Last Lutanist. DEAN B. LYMAN, JR.
16. Battle-Retrospect. AMOS NIVEN WILDER
17. Silver Wands. MARION M. BOYD
18. Mosaics. BEATRICE E. HARMON
19. Up and Down. ELIZABETH JESSUP BLAKE
20. Coach into Pumpkin. DOROTHY E. REID
21. Quest. ELEANOR SLATER
22. High Passage. THOMAS HORNSBY FERRIL
23. Dark Pavilion. LINDLEY WILLIAMS HUBBELL
24. Twist o' Smoke. MILDRED BOWERS
25. A Stranger and Afraid. TED OLSON
26. This Unchanging Mask. FRANCIS CLAIBORNE MASON
27. Hemlock Wall. FRANCES M. FROST
28. Half-Light and Overtones. HENRI FAUST
29. Virtuosa: A Book of Verse. LOUISE OWEN
30. Dark Certainty. DOROTHY BELLE FLANAGAN
31. Worn Earth. PAUL H. ENGLE

92

32. Dark Hills Under. SHIRLEY BARKER
33. Permit Me Voyage. JAMES AGEE
34. Theory of Flight. MURIEL RUKEYSER
35. The Deer Come Down. EDWARD WEISMILLER
36. The Gardener Mind. MARGARET HALEY
37. Letter to a Comrade. JOY DAVIDMAN
38. The Connecticut River and Other Poems. REUEL DENNEY
39. Return Again, Traveler. NORMAN ROSTEN
40. The Metaphysical Sword. J. INGALLS
41. For My People. M. WALKER
42. Love Letter from an Impossible Land. W. MEREDITH
43. Cut Is the Branch. C. E. BUTLER
44. Family Circle. E. MERRIAM
45. Poems. JOAN MURRAY
46. A Beginning. R. HORAN
47. The Grasshopper's Man and Other Poems. ROSALIE MOORE
48. A Change of World. ADRIENNE CECILE RICH
49. A Mask for Janus. W. S. MERWIN
50. Various Jangling Keys. EDGAR BOGARDUS
51. An Armada of Thirty Whales. DANIEL G. HOFFMAN
52. Some Trees. JOHN L. ASHBERY
53. The Green Wall. JAMES WRIGHT

VOLUMES 41 AND 46–53 ARE IN PRINT.